MINDFUL Me

Lifeskills Journal

For Cool, Calm, Confident Kids

First published by Simone Derman, 2022

Copyright © 2021 Simone Derman

ISBN: 978-0-6397-2532-1

Interior layout, illustration and typesetting by
Gregg Davies Media (www.greggdavies.com)
All rights reserved.

Notes for PARENTS

- -

This journal is designed to introduce your child to an understanding of how emotions work, how they can be managed and celebrated, and how they can use mindfulness techniques to unleash the superhero that is hidden inside them.

Depending on your child's independence and literacy levels, you can help them to work through the journal; or let them work through it on their own, asking for help when they feel they need it.

Allow your child to lead in their progress through the journal: they will get the most benefit from it if they are excited and enthusiastic about their journaling sessions.

What's Inside This Journal?

Getting Started With Your Journal

- - - - - - - - - - - - - - - - - -

Every person on Earth has a superhero inside of them waiting to be unleashed, but sometimes they appear to be hiding! This journal will take you on a journey of self-discovery to help you unlock your secret superhero with a series of activities, exercises and recommendations that will help you become the best possible version of yourself.

This is YOUR journal. You can ask an adult or journal buddy to help you if you want to, or you can color in the pictures, scribble on the pages, go through the journal in order, or jump about: whatever you prefer.

Before you begin to get to know your secret superhero, you must first learn all about someone you may hardly know yet: YOURSELF!

Name: _____

2

All About Me

Best friends

Pets

Hobbies

 favorite CANDY

favorite Movie

My Family

favorite PLACE

favorite color

 CRAYON

favorite Music

My Birthday

favorite BOOKS to read

favorite VACATION

favorite class in school

favorite food

Draw a picture of yourself. Use a photograph (on a tablet or cellphone) or a mirror, whichever you prefer and draw in all the things that make you YOU. If you like, you can paste a photograph of yourself here too.

Everyone is different in all sorts of ways. Some of these ways are physical, while others are not. Here is where you celebrate what is unique about you.

Hair color: _____   Classroom or Gym? _____

Eye color: _____   Summer or winter? _____

Tall or short? _____

Your Family Tree

Grandparent   Grandparent   Grandparent   Grandparent

Parent   Parent

YOU!

Your YOUniqueness

What makes you different from others?

_____

_____

What makes you the same as others?

_____

_____

Use your imaginations to fill in the clouds below.

If I made a movie, it would be about:

If I wrote a book, the topic would be:

If I invented something, it would be:

My Superpowers

As you get to know yourself better, you will discover that everyone is born with unique strengths. Sometimes these are obvious: being able to draw well without being taught, singing beautifully, or being really good at sport (but everyone needs to practice, no matter how much natural talent they have!).

Sometimes you need to work very hard to find your strengths, which might be more 'strength of character' than talent. Being patient, kind, and brave are all strengths too. Complete the wordsearch puzzle on the next page to see some other examples of strengths.

Wordsearch Puzzle

```
G C Q I E F Y W V G E E U S H
N R C Y D N I T H W Y O F L T
E E S M V S T A I O U L D K H
G A M U D N G H X S N Z E V I
E T N O P L C A U R O E G V Q
C I M K I N D N E S S I S L B
O V P P A Z Y G V T I C R T D
U I E A P R A H N I R A W U Y
R T W C E H K E Y B G M S K C
A Y N V A B M Z U E W M U M Z
G U A S N G D U E C Q V C T J
E R R Z D Z N K A W V U N V E
B W H U A Z T M V Z U Y C U U
U A J S F E K L F M I J I P V
L O V E O F L E A R N I N G Y
```

Curiosity	Kindness
Honesty	Enthusiasm
Courage	Creativity
Love of Learning	Bravery
Wisdom	Judgment

Journalling:
Getting Started

Journaling is a great way to record how you feel and note down what has happened in your day. It is a wonderful tool which helps you to become more aware of your feelings, and also to grow your superhero powers!

Complete the journal page, using the prompts. You can fill in a journal page every day, every week, or whenever you like. Do try to do it regularly: this will be helpful to you, and it will soon become routine.

(There are spare journal pages at the back of the book!)

TODAY IS:

Draw your day in this box.

Write a little about your day. Try to include three GOOD things!

Date: ___ / ___ / ___

Today I feel:

Sad   Angry   Sick   Meh

Okay   All Right   Pretty Good   Good   Awesome!

Because: _____
_____
_____

Three GOOD things that happened today!

1 _____ 2 _____ 3 _____

Today: I am GRATEFUL for:
_____
_____
_____

Tomorrow: I am LOOKING FORWARD to:
_____
_____
_____

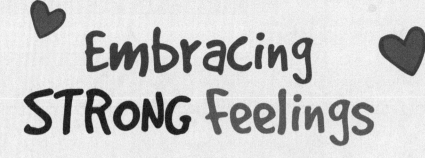

Embracing STRONG feelings

It can be hard to deal with some emotions because they bring forth certain feelings in your body, making you feel uncomfortable and overwhelmed. This journal will help you to cope with these tricky feelings. Being able to embrace and accept your feelings is only possible when you understand what emotions you are feeling and why you are feeling them.

DAY OF THE WEEK: / /

Today I felt:

HAPPY!   LOVED!   EXCITED!

ANNOYED   WORRIED   SAD

_____   _____ AND _____

Three GOOD things about today were:

_____

_____

Something that made me laugh:

_____

_____

Something INTERESTING I learned today:

_____

_____

13

How to work through strong feelings:

Step 1 -
NAME THE EMOTION
Ask - what am I feeling?
Answer - I am angry and a bit sad.

Step 2 -
IDENTIFY THE CAUSE
Ask - why am I feeling this way? What happened?
Answer - I didn't get an A in math, and I tried really hard!

Step 3 -
WHERE CAN I FEEL THE FEELING IN MY BODY
Ask - where is the feeling showing up in my body? Are my palms sweaty? Is my heart racing?
Answer - I can feel it in my eyes and throat (I want to cry) and in my chest, like a lump.

Step 4 -
ACCEPT THE FEELING
Welcome the feeling
Okay, I am upset because I have had a disappointment.

Step 5 -
CHALLENGE THE EMOTION
Ask - Is my emotion appropriate to the situation and what message is it giving me? What lesson can I learn from this for the future?

Should I be disappointed? Yes, I can be disappointed that my hard work didn't pay off. I could stay sad about it; or I can try harder next time or ask my teacher for help so I ace the next test!

TODAY'S DATE: _____ / _____ / _____

One great thing happened today! It was _____

_____

_____

_____

TODAY I FELT:

Angry | Happy | Sad | Confused | Scared | Excited

Sick | Sad | Loved | Joyful | Exited | Shocked

TODAY:

- I was CURIOUS
- I SOLVED a problem
- I WORKED on something difficult
- I ASKED for help
- I SLEPT well
- _____

TODAY I FELT:

TODAY IS: _____

Draw your day in this box.

Write a little about your day. Try to include three GOOD things!

_____
_____
_____
_____

Introspection:
Self-Awareness

Welcoming your feelings means that you can notice them without trying to judge them or ignore them. This is very useful as sometimes, if we think we're not allowed to be angry or sad, we then feel guilty or bad too! But if we welcome our feelings, no matter what they are, we can understand what we are feeling and learn ways to deal with them.

Knowing how different parts of your brain work and why they do certain things can help you deal with big emotions.

The brain is part of your nervous system. Along with the spinal cord, it connects to all the nerves that run through your body. So, for example, when you touch something cold or see a pretty sunset, that information travels through your body and into your brain. This information helps you understand what is happening around you and how to respond.

The brain also uses those nerves to tell muscles what to do. So your brain sends the signals, your muscles receive them, and suddenly you run, swim or talk.

The nervous system consists of millions of neurons, which are microscopic cells. They can join together with other neurons to form connections called pathways that transmit information.
These pathways get stronger the more you practice something.
For example, learning how to ride a bike shows how neurons form pathways. The first time you try may seem very hard. You have to think about how to move and balance, but the more you practice, the stronger the pathways become, and eventually, you don't even have to think much about how to ride your bike. It becomes automatic.

The brain can be divided into two parts to help you understand. They are called the "Thinking Brain" and the "Emotional Brain."

The "Thinking Brain" is much more sophisticated than the "Emotional Brain." It consists of the Prefrontal Cortex and various other parts. The Prefrontal Cortex behind the forehead is the part of the brain responsible for helping us focus, learn, plan, and solve problems. It also helps us make good decisions.

The Pre-frontal Cortex also sends and receives memories to and from the Hippocampus, which is like a library that stores memories and skills we have learned.

The "Emotional Brain" is where our feelings come from. This is where the amygdala lives. It is like a superhero which tries to protect us and keep us safe all the time. Sometimes it can mistake stress for real threats and that can stop the "Thinking Brain" from getting the information it needs to make good choices.
When the amygdala is upset, the hippocampus also cannot store any memories or information.

This is sometimes why it's so hard for us to listen to instructions when we are upset and angry. The hippocampus also can't recall any memories or previously learnt skills when we are upset or angry. Simply put, this means that sometimes having strong emotions can stop us from thinking clearly. This is why learning mindfulness and skills to calm ourselves down when we have big feelings can help us think more clearly and make better decisions.

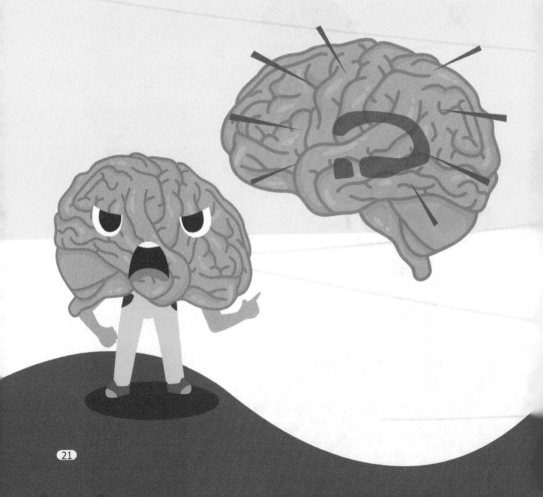

If you can think about what kind of situations cause you to feel a certain way, this can help you avoid situations you don't like in future and recreate those situations that leave you feeling happy.

Step 1 - Identify the situation
Step 2 - Identify the feeling
Step 3 - Avoid or recreate the feeling for the future

Think of some times when you felt a strong emotion.

EXAMPLE:

What Happened?
My brother went into my room and took my toys without asking.

What Can i do about it
Ask my brother to ask first next time.

How i felt
I felt angry

NOW ITS YOUR TURN:

What Happened?
_____
_____

What Can i do about it
_____
_____

How i felt
_____
_____

TODAY'S DATE: _____ / _____ / _____

One great thing happened today! It was _____
_____
_____
_____

TODAY I FELT:

TODAY:

I was CURIOUS

I SOLVED a problem

I WORKED on something difficult

I ASKED for help

I SLEPT well

_____

Things I can do to ground myself when I have big feelings

A good exercise is to imagine yourself lying on your back under a tree on the grass staring up at the sky. Each feeling is a like a cloud in the sky. You can see the clouds (the feelings) approaching and passing. When they do, describe them by naming the feeling, or maybe give it a color (red for anger or yellow for joy) — and you can tell it to go away and thank it for the message. Or you can wait: just acknowledge it and sit with the feeling.

Fill the clouds below with your emotions and give them the message you would like to give your emotions. Or just sit quietly and imagine that you are lying in that field, looking up at the clouds and the sky, at peace with yourself – and your feelings.

Soon, you will be able to say how you are feeling all the time, and that means that people can help you, if you need them to.

DAY OF THE WEEK: / /

Today I felt:

HAPPY! **LOVED!** **EXCITED!**

ANNOYED **WORRIED** **SAD**

_____ _____ AND _____

Three GOOD things about today were:

_____

_____

Something that made me laugh:

_____

_____

Something INTERESTING I learned today:

_____

_____

The Feel Wheel!

- -

The Feel Wheel is another tool that you can use to help you dig a little deeper into what you are feeling when a big feeling happens.

Storytime: The Power of Positive Thinking!

Billy was grumpy. He wished he could swim as well as Marina, but he couldn't. That's what he told himself, anyway. But every week at swimming practice, Billy would 'forget' his swimsuit and go and play video games under a shady tree.

"Come and swim!" Marina would call.

"I'm tired!" Billy would say, or "I didn't bring my swimsuit."

But Marina went to every practice, and she was chosen to be part of the championship team.

"That's not fair!" said Billy. "I wanted to be on the team."

Coach overheard Billy saying this. "Marina wanted to be on the team, too," he told Billy. "At first, I told her 'no' because she wasn't very good and needed more practice."

"What?" Billy was astonished. "That's what you said to me at the beginning of the year."

"That's right," said Coach. "I told you both 'no' on the same day. But do you know what Marina did?"

Billy nodded his head: "She went home and cried. I know that because she told me so."

"But then, she dried her face, went on the Internet, and researched how to become a better swimmer. She got fitter. She researched videos on using better techniques. She got better at kicking her feet straight and hard. And she watched dozens of swimming events to see how it all worked."

"Oh," said Billy, blushing red.

Coach nodded. "You can see where this is going, can't you? You both wanted to be on the swim team, but Marina is the one who worked out how to achieve that dream."

Billy went home that day filled with a determination to be as good as Marina. He went out for a run, but got very tired after two blocks, so he stopped and walked home. He decided he would do exercises in his bedroom instead of running. He did ten jumping jacks.

"Gosh," he said, "I'm really hot and tired."

He did ten sit-ups.

"Ow!" he moaned. "My tummy hurts."

He thought he would do ten push-ups. He got into position.
"Ow, my arms are sore," he said to himself. He lowered himself into the first push-up... and stayed down! As hard as he tried, he couldn't push himself back up!
Billy was filled with sadness and began to cry. "I just want to swim really well," he sobbed. "Why is it so hard?"
Then Billy felt silly for crying and began to scold himself.

"You're stupid, Billy," he said. "You're a crybaby."
Billy's mom heard him and knocked on his door.
"What's going on?" she asked.
"I'm stupid and lazy and I'll never be on the swim team," burst out
Billy. He explained what Coach had told him.
"I didn't know you wanted to join the swim team," said Billy's mom.
"Well, I do!" he said, a little rudely.

Billy's mom looked at him and saw he was upset, so she didn't discipline him for his outburst. Instead, she gave him a hug.

"Billy, you've only just started trying to get fit. It's not easy and it's only your first day."

"But Marina's done it!"

"Marina worked very hard to get fit. At first, she couldn't do it either. Her mom told me."

But Billy didn't really believe his mom. "Well, maybe I don't want to be on the team after all," he said grumpily. "I'm happy with my video games."

Will Billy keep going? Or will he quit?

The next day, Billy put on his workout clothes. He stood by the front door, trying to decide if he should try running again or if he should do exercises in his room. But secretly, Billy was thinking that if he "couldn't" decide within fifteen minutes, he would give up and go and play his video game. He tried to push that secret thought away, but it kept coming back.

The clock ticked past five minutes. Ten minutes. Eleven minutes. At twelve minutes, the doorbell rang! Billy jumped and opened it.

"Oh, that was quick!" said Marina.

"Marina," said Billy. "What are you doing here?"

"Coach told me you were still interested in being on the swim team. I can help you train if you like?"

"Oh," muttered Billy, going red with embarrassment.

"I don't know if I even want to be on the team anymore."
"Nonsense!" said Marina. "You're in your workout clothes, and you've been standing by the door. You're obviously going to work out. If you really didn't want to do it, you wouldn't have bothered changing."
Billy glanced up, realizing Marina was right. "Okay," he muttered. "I do want to be on the team but getting fit is so hard."

"I'm so unfit and can't run more than a block, and I can't do a push-up—"

"Oh, hush!" said Marina energetically. "I was exactly the same. I was so disappointed when Coach said 'no' that I thought I would never swim again. But then I realized I loved swimming and would do anything to be good at it. That first day, I ran only a block and felt terrible."

"The next day, I ran three blocks and felt all right. By the end of the week, I was so tired, but the running was easier. Come on, I'll run with you."

"Will you really?" asked Billy hopefully.

"Yes," said Marina. "Every day, if you want me to."

A moment later, the sound of two pairs of feet running down the road could be heard.

How will it turn out? Read on to find out!

After two months, Coach pinned an announcement to the noticeboard. He was going to hold tryouts for the swim meet that was coming up! Marina saw the notice and told Billy.

"Oh no!" said Billy. "I'm not ready."

"Yes, you are," said Marina calmly. "You can run as fast as me for as long as me. You can do all the swimming strokes — some of them even better than me, in fact. And you completely understand how to pace yourself because of all the swim meets and YouTube videos we've watched together. You've got this."

Swim Team Tryouts! Monday!'

"Okay..." said Billy, a little uncertainly.

"Come on," said Marina. "You've worked so hard, I'm sure you'll do well."

"Really?" asked Billy. "I don't feel like anything has changed!"

"Shut your eyes for a moment."

Billy did so as Marina put her hands on his shoulders and guided him to the mirror.

"Imagine yourself standing there as you were two months ago. Can you remember?"

Billy frowned. "Yeah. Uh — I was unfit and slouched a bit. I looked pale and unhealthy because I didn't go out much. I was tired all the time. Um, my hair was longer — I cut it when I started swimming because it got in my eyes. What else?"

"That's fine," said Marina. "Now, keep that image of yourself in your head. Can you see the old you?"

"Yes," said Billy.

"Now open your eyes."

Billy opened his eyes and gasped. He looked very different now. He looked fit and healthy, and his skin was smooth and clear. He was taller, he thought! But maybe that was because he wasn't slouching any more. He stood up straight, and his eyes sparkled with interest. He looked very different from the Billy of a few months before!

"I think you are," said Marina, when he mentioned that he seemed taller. "But you also stand up straighter now. Your posture is much better — you always used to stare at the ground. Now you lift your head and look at people."

Billy stared at his changed self. "Wow…" he said softly. "I didn't realize I'd changed that much. But now…" He smiled. "I think I really can make it onto the team."

On tryouts day, Billy lined up with the other hopefuls. He came first in his two favorite strokes: front crawl and backstroke. Afterwards, he climbed out of the pool and looked at Coach hopefully.
Coach didn't say anything: he just held his hand up for a high five. Bewildered, Billy glanced at Marina, who was sitting on the side of the pool, watching. She gave him a double thumbs-up, and he grinned broadly, hastily high-fiving Coach.
"Welcome to the team, Billy," said Coach.

Watch out for the next Storytime, when there will be a brand-new story for you to read along with and learn.

Lateral Thinking Skills

- - - - - - - - - - - - - - - - - - - -

Using the skills you have learned in How Am I Feeling and the Feel Wheel, can you identify some of Billy's feelings throughout the story?

Write them down below.

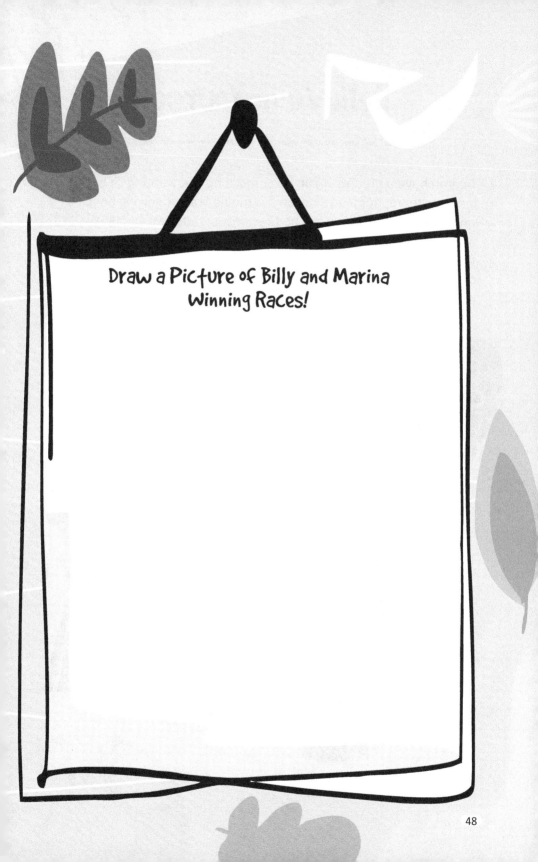

Draw a Picture of Billy and Marina
Winning Races!

Believe in Yourself

Do you have a dream? It can be something like wanting to be on a sports team, hoping to become a movie star, or getting an A on a math test. Dreams can be big or little, but they are always important. Sometimes other people can dismiss your dreams, and that hurts, even if they are just joking. It is your dream and if you are serious about it, ignore what others are saying and work towards achieving it.

In the space below or on a separate sheet of paper, draw a picture of yourself. Imagine already having achieved your dream. Are you older and surrounded by all the bestselling books you wrote? Are you the sportsperson who won the game for the team? Or are you a celebrated scientist who has created a cure which saved lives? Underneath the picture, write the words: "My dream is to _____." And fill in the missing word or words.

But — and this is an important but — you will almost always have to work hard to achieve your dream. It doesn't matter how far away your dream is, you can begin to work towards it now, showing everyone that you are serious about it. More importantly, you are showing yourself that you can do it! This is the power of believing in yourself!

Date: ___ / ___ / ___

 **Today I feel:**

 Sad
 Angry
 Sick
 Meh

 Okay
 All Right
 Pretty Good
 Good
 Awesome!

Because:
_____
_____

Three GOOD things that happened today!

1_____ 2_____ 3_____

Today: I am GRATEFUL for:
_____
_____

Tomorrow: I am LOOKING FORWARD to:
_____
_____
_____

51

Make a Feel-Good Playlist!

Make a playlist of songs that make you feel happy, energized, and ready for anything!

Here are some to get you started – add your own favorites underneath:
Never Say Never – Justin Bieber
Fight Song – Rachel Platten
Me – Taylor Swift
Can't Stop the Feeling – Justin Timberlake

Create a vision board

You will need a large sheet of cardboard and some old magazines that you are allowed to cut up. At the top, write down the dream you would like to achieve. Let us say that you want to be a scientist. Find scientific words in the magazine's headlines. Look for images of people working in science labs or doing research on the topics in which you are interested. Draw sketches of yourself learning hard. Then, somewhere on the board or on your page, write down what you need to do to make your dream happen. If you are not sure, go on the Internet — ask someone you trust to help you — and do some research.

Go on: What's Your Dream?

Growth Mindset: What it is and how to get one!

What does it mean to have a growth mindset?

If you want to be an author, you have to read many books, write down stories and ideas, and practice your spelling and grammar.

If you want to be an artist, you must draw and paint often to stay in good practice.

And scientists keep learning about their subject throughout their careers.

If you want to be on the sports team, you must be fit and know how to play the game — but you must also be a good team member, being kind and supportive and respecting the other players and your coach.

If you want to be a famous movie star or model, you will have to look after your health and do things like take part in the school play — even if you don't get the lead role right away!

In short, you need a Growth Mindset! This means understanding that there are many steps along the way to reach your goal and that, with a positive and persistent attitude, you can overcome any challenges in your way. People with a growth mindset don't give up the first time things don't go their way.

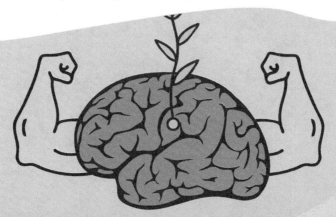

Remember the Thinking Brain and the Feeling Brain from earlier? Having a Growth Mindset means using your Thinking Brain to work out how you feel, and why – and then using those emotions to help you GROW.

Inside you, your secret superhero will show you how strong and capable you really are.
But beware of the Kryptonite of the fixed mindset: it will try to shrink your Growth Mindset. Your secret superhero says: I will try; I can do it; I will work at it.
The supervillain's Kryptonite says: you can't; you will fail; why even bother?

DAY OF THE WEEK: / /

Today I felt:

HAPPY!   LOVED!   EXCITED!

ANNOYED   WORRIED   SAD

_____ _____ AND _____

Three GOOD things about today were:

_____

_____

Something that made me laugh:

_____

_____

Something INTERESTING I learned today:

_____

_____

Change your

thoughts

and you can change

The world!

We all have negative thoughts, and they can make us feel really uncomfortable. Sometimes they can be really hard to get rid of once they are in your head, but here are some secrets to beating negative thoughts.

Learn to question your thoughts! Is it a fact?
When a tricky icky thought pops into your head......Ask yourself, "Is this true? Is this really, really the truth?" More often than not, we feel that things are much worse than they really are.

Questioning your thoughts helps create some space between you and your thoughts, allowing you to put some distance between the negativity and the truth.

For example, you may have missed scoring a goal at soccer practice, leaving you feeling disappointed in yourself. This can lead to the negative thought "I never score for my team, I'm a terrible striker!" Now, stop! Question your thought. Is this true? Have you really never scored any goals during practice, ever?
Are you really a terrible striker or are you just feeling disappointed for missing one goal?
You will most likely find that you are not terrible: you are just having one bad day.

What would you tell a friend who was having this thought? Would you agree with them or try make them feel better and turn their thought around into a positive one? Be as kind to yourself as you would your best friend.

Ask yourself if this negative thought will even matter in 5 years or 5 months from now.

Next, you can train your brain to always reach for the next best thought. It can seem unrealistic to try and go from a negative thought to an extremely positive one in just a few seconds.

But like steps on a ladder, you can always just reach for the next best thought to get out of your negative fixed mindset.

THEN

I have SAVINGS!

I will save 10% of my allowance, no matter what:

I will open a savings account:

I will ask parents /carer for help:

Can't save my allowance:

NOW

THEN

I AM good at sport!

I will work hard for six months:

Will find a sport I like – that will make it easier to do often:

Will try harder in gym class:

Not good at any sport:

NOW

THEN

I LIKE the way I look!

I will be as kind to myself as I would be to a stranger:

I will learn to love the parts I like: I will say, 'I am good enough' in the mirror every morning:

I will find three things I like about myself (good hair, pretty eyes, strong legs; nice teeth):

I hate the way I look:

NOW

Positive Affirmations

Did you know that saying kind phrases about yourself out loud can help you to chase away the negative thoughts?
These kind phrases are called affirmations and the more we practice saying them to ourselves, the better we will feel.
Look in the mirror, give yourself a high five and highlight all those that feel true for you on the next page.

Feel free to add your own affirmations at the end of the list in the blank spaces provided.

I am clever
I am kind
I have a BIG imagination
I tell funny jokes
I am a good leader
I am a good friend
I am determined
I am unique
I am brave
I try new things all the time
I build well
I am artistic
Now you can think of some things that make you super!

I am _____

I am good at _____

I always _____

A little earlier we mentioned how a Fixed Mindset can upset your Growth Mindset. Let's explore this in more detail.
A Growth Mindset, we have learned, is all about being open to learning, trying hard, and not giving up.

But what is a Fixed Mindset?
A Fixed Mindset is what happens when negative thoughts win.
But the good news is that a Fixed Mindset can become a Growth Mindset.

Let's look at some ways you can change your thinking and language to create a Growth Mindset.

A Fixed Mindset says:

I can't do it...

I already know...

I give up...

I don't listen to useful feedback...

I'm dumb, I'll never be able to...

I can't help it...

I don't need practice...

If I don't get it right straight away, I stop trying...

I don't want to try...

I'll never be any good at this...

A Growth Mindset says:

I will learn how...

I am willing to learn...

I will keep trying...

I will learn from feedback...

I can do it; I must just try harder...

I can do better...

I need the practice...

I am determined to keep trying...

I am willing to try...

I will get better...

A Fixed Mindset puts you in a locked box, but a Growth Mindset is like a key that will unlock all the possibilities that life has to offer.

The best way to transform your Fixed Mindset Kryptonite into Superhero Can-Do Magic is by using the right words. Did you notice how many times the words 'don't,' 'never,' and 'can't' were used in the Fixed Mindset list? Nearly all of them were negative, weren't they? A little later we will meet 'I can't' who is one of the biggest supervillains out there, but for now, we will work on changing negative statements into positive possibilities.

Now you write some Growth Mindset phrases for things that you want to achieve:

_____

_____

_____

Getting out of Your comfort Zone

When you are young, you can be a little scared of everything, but also interested in everything, because it is all so new to you. As you grow up, some things become familiar to you: your family, your friends, your school, and some places in your town. You get used to doing some things, and you like them, because they are known. All these things are in what is called your "comfort zone".

Your comfort zone can be a real place (parts of your town that you know very well) but it is also a headspace. In the headspace, your comfort zone is made up of all the things you like to do and have done many times before: sleeping over with your best friend, playing basketball or baseball, swimming in the town pool. Outside of your comfort zone (both kinds of comfort zone) are all the things that you don't know so much about.

Getting out of your comfort zone can be scary: doing strange things, meeting strange people, perhaps making mistakes or getting things wrong — many people like to stay inside their comfort zones, even adults!

But it is okay to make mistakes when we are trying new things. If no one were ever wrong, we wouldn't learn very much about anything!

Color in the two zones, and then fill in your favorite comfort zone things: watching TV, going for a walk with your parents, having a sleep-over with your best friend.

Next fill in some 'Out of Your Comfort Zone' lines: These are things you still want to learn or do. Things like learning to swim, learning a foreign language, or signing up for a school camping trip.

Out of Your Comfort Zone: Where the FUN happens!

COMFORT ZONE

Thomas Edison invented the lightbulb and he tried nearly one hundred filaments before he found one that worked well. He didn't think of it as making mistakes: he found nearly one hundred ways that didn't work, and that allowed him to work out what would work!

He needed to get it wrong — many times! — before he got it right. If he had stayed in his comfort zone, you would be working through this journal by candlelight!

Can you think of some good reasons for staying in your comfort zone and some good reasons for getting out of it?

Stay In:

_____

_____

Get Out!

_____

_____

Some reasons that you might have for staying in your comfort zone could include being safe; knowing everyone and everything; not being embarrassed by not knowing something; and avoiding stress. Some reasons that you might have for getting out of your comfort zone could include learning new things; being comfortable in a wide range of places and activities; meeting new people who will become friends; having a more exciting life; having the confidence to cope with new situations.

There's no such thing as failing!
Fail just means: First Attempt in Learning!

F - FIRST
A - ATTEMPT
I - IN
L - LEARNING

And finally, if you get out of your comfort zone and do many new things, you become comfortable with all those things, so you have a much bigger comfort zone when you do want to take things easy for a little while! It can be very hard to take the first steps on a new path, but once you begin, it gets easier. Before long, you will look back on your "old" self and wonder why you were so worried about taking that all-important first step!

Celebrate Your Successes

Every time you make a mistake, write the mistake on a slip of paper, and put it in a jar. Use different colored pieces of paper so it looks colorful. BUT don't just write the mistake down: write down what you learned from it, too. Be like Edison. Instead of saying, "I made a mistake," he would have written down, "Today, I discovered that straw does not make a good light bulb filament."

This way, your "mistake jar" actually becomes your "celebration" jar. When your jar is full, CELEBRATE all the lessons you have learned!

The first time I made cookies, I used salt instead of sugar! I learned that cookies taste much better when they are sweet!

I dropped my cup and spilled my juice. I learned that it is better to carry my juice to the dining table first, then my snack-plate, and to be slow and careful!

I tripped over my backpack and bumped my knee. I learned that it is better to put my backpack in its correct place every time!

Now you do some:

- _____
  _____
  _____

- _____
  _____
  _____

- _____
  _____

Resilience:
How to Keep Going

Today's world moves superfast. If you order something online, it's there in a matter of days, if not hours. If you want to speak to someone on the other side of the globe, you can email or phone them immediately. If you feel like takeout in the middle of the night, you can have it. If you enjoy a television series, you can watch it all in a day or two. (In earlier times, you had to wait a whole week for the next episode to find out what happened next!)

All this speed means that people are forgetting how to be patient. They become impatient and grumpy, and sometimes they complain or cancel their order.

And that's very sad, because there is something lovely about anticipation.

That means waiting patiently, looking forward to the things arriving or the event happening, and enjoying the wait.

It can also mean taking your time and working towards a goal, whether it is saving a little money every month, taking a lesson or two every week, or reading a page or a chapter a day. There is a saying: "It's not about the destination, it's about the journey." This saying is about being patient and enjoying the small things and rewards that happen along the way.

If you are negative and miserable while you are waiting for something to happen, not only will you feel bad, but everyone around you will feel bad, too. Being patient is another way of being polite. But it is also a way of working towards achieving your dreams and finding your secret superhero!

Remember the picture you drew of yourself when you first started the journal? It's time to draw yourself again. This time, think of all the things you have learned about your dreams and how to achieve them, and getting out of your comfort zone.

Draw yourself doing something that you are very proud of having tried — even if you weren't very good at it!

Learning from Mistakes

In our first Storytime, Billy changed from having a poor mindset to having a positive mental attitude! He did this because Marina helped him develop a Growth Mindset.

Remember all the words from the puzzle on page 10? They are all positive words, all about learning and growing and freeing your secret superhero!

Everyone can have a Growth Mindset if they want to — all you have to do is put the words "I can't" in jail!

Pretend "I can't" is a supervillain. He's really mean and stomps around saying mean things to people, calling them names and making them feel bad. Just like any other bully, though, "I can't" backs off when somebody stronger stands up to him. "Yet" is a word that makes "I can't" behave. And in fact, the only time "I can't" is allowed out of jail is when he is accompanied by "yet"!
Do you get it?

I CANT YET

What this means is that you shouldn't say "I can't" when you are learning new things. If Mom says, "Let's go swimming," you're not tempted to say, "I can't swim." But what you can say is: "But Mom! I can't swim… yet." "I can't" always says no. "I can't" won't even try. But "yet" makes it okay not to have done something, because "yet" means that you are willing to try and do what it takes to learn that new thing. Do you see how that makes a big difference?

"I can't" has friends who are supervillains just like him! These are negative words that try to make you feel too small or unready to try new things. But, just like "I can't," these supervillains can be tamed with the power of YET! Some of these villainous friends are: "I don't want to," "I don't like," "It's too hard," and "I give up"!

Write down some things that "I can't" and his friends tell you, then help your secret superhero flip the switch in your brain that makes everything possible, by writing "yet" next to all of them, even if you have to be an adult to do them. It's never too early to have a dream, remember?

Example: I can't write neatly with a pen (flip!) YET! I am working on my letter shapes.

I _____ (flip!) _____

I _____ (flip!) _____

I _____ (flip!) _____

I _____ (flip!) _____

I _____ (flip!) _____

There are five lines for things that you can't do yet. That seems like a lot, doesn't it? But it's really not — the happiest people keep on learning all their lives!

Growing Your Growth Mindset

Do you feel like one of those people who always struggles? You want to draw beautifully, but the pencil won't quite do what you want it to? Or you'd love to learn a different language, but you feel silly saying words that sound unfamiliar? Or perhaps you feel very self-conscious and worry that people will laugh if you try out for the team or dance in front of them.

Did you know that almost everyone in the whole world has felt like that at one time or another? Yes, even the people who you admire for being clever or sporty or successful at everything they try! How did they do it? With a positive mental attitude and by having a Growth Mindset! Color in the picture overleaf and see how many kinds of secret superheroes there really are!

Knowing What You Are Feeling

We have looked at emotions and have learned how to identify and express them. But sometimes our feelings can stop our Growth Mindset and so stop us from living our best life. Let us look at some ways to be in control of our feelings, even the ones that make us feel sad or not so good.

Some feelings are hot: anger, excitement, and surprise; while others are cold: worry, sadness, and fear. What are the feelings that are stopping your Growth Mindset? Write down the emotion, and then color in the part of your body where you can feel that emotion. For example: If you really want to learn to ride a horse, but you are scared of being so high up in the air, your hands might become clammy, your heart might beat hard, and you might feel your breath catch in your throat.

color the places you feel these emotions.

Sad – Blue

Fear – Black   Guilt – Brown

Anger – Red   Jealous – Green

Nervous – orange   Happy – Yellow

Embrace that feeling! Sometimes we are told to fight our feelings — but that can make it worse. Instead of trying to ignore your feelings, acknowledge them. I am scared. I am angry. I am sad. (Also remember to acknowledge positive emotions too! I am happy. I am strong. I am brave.)

Allow yourself to understand why you feel the emotion that you do. For example: I am afraid of riding a horse because I might fall off and hurt myself.

Now you have acknowledged the feeling and understand what your body is telling you, you can overcome the problem. Just like "I can't" isn't allowed out of jail unless "Yet" is with him, you can find a way to overcome your problem. Your feelings about a situation shouldn't stop you from achieving your dream!

By acknowledging your feelings, you can find solutions, and by sharing your feelings, others can help you come up with solutions you may not have thought about yet.

You can ask to ride a smaller horse. You can tell your riding teacher that you are scared of getting hurt and they will give you a helmet to keep your head safe, a padded jacket to protect your body, and they will also teach you how to fall safely. (Yes, that is really a thing! You can learn to fall safely!)

Managing Feelings

If there are two emotions that the supervillains love, they are fear and anger. Fear often makes us quiet and still, but anger can make us shout, fight, and maybe even break things. This can get us into trouble, so while anger is acknowledged and welcomed like the other emotions, it must be managed, too. This does not mean you cannot show anger or tell others that you are angry. It simply means that you must try not to hurt anyone when you are angry, by saying mean things to them or hitting them. Feeling angry is not an excuse for unacceptable actions.

Breathing and meditation are wonderful exercises for helping you to stay in control of your mood. Meditation is sometimes called "mindfulness" and that is a good name for it: having a mind full of calm. It is easy to meditate, and you can do it almost anywhere.

Find a quiet place where you will not be disturbed for fifteen minutes or so. Sit or lie down comfortably and relax. Some people sit cross-legged, while others lie flat on their back. Close your eyes and place your hands on your tummy, just above your belly button. Next we will practise some Box breathing. Box breathing is a type of rhythmic breathing where you follow a pattern to help you stay focused and calm.

In your comfortable position with your hands on your tummy, slowly breathe in for 4 seconds, hold your breath for 4 seconds, then slowly release your breathe for 4 seconds and hold for another 4 seconds before repeating.

Every time you breathe out, throw one of your worries out of your head. Do this for three to five minutes or until all of your worries and anger have been banished — sometimes you might need to banish them a few times!

When your head is calm and empty, keep your deep, calm breathing going and just exist. Don't try to think about anything at all. As your meditation time comes to an end, breathe in all the positive emotions and feelings you can think of.

Now you are calmer, you can use empathy to understand why people might say or do things that have upset or frightened you. Empathy is thinking about things from other people's point of view, and it is a superpower that anyone can learn. If someone says or does something, try to think why they might do it. If you are tempted to tease someone, stop before you go ahead, and think about how being teased in that way would make you feel.

For example, calling someone with long hair "Rapunzel" is not an insult and it can be funny. That would be a good tease.

Calling someone with a big nose "Giant Schnoz" is rude, and it might hurt the feelings of the person. They almost certainly know that their nose is on the large side, and they might be very self-conscious about it.

If you use empathy to understand other people, and meditation to transform your feelings into positives, your Growth Mindset will become stronger than ever! Two Growth Mindset case studies are up next.

Afroz Shah:
The Man Who Cleaned the Beach
A Growth Mindset Case Study

In 2015, Afroz Shah, a young and ambitious lawyer, moved into a wonderful new apartment overlooking Versova Beach in Mumbai. But when he looked down at the beach from his flat, he was horrified. The beach was terribly littered — so covered in trash that the sand could not be seen at all! In fact, the trash was so thick that it was inches deep.

"I should do something about this," he said, and along with a neighbor, he began to go to the beach, picking up bags full of soggy paper, plastic bottles, cans, and all sorts of yucky stuff. People would look at him, then look at the whole beach and say, "Why do you bother? There's so much of it!"

But Afroz didn't let that get him down and carried on.

Slowly, he began to attract attention and admiration from other people who would come and help him for a few hours at a time. He called the local municipality (that's like a local council), and they agreed to send garbage trucks to come and remove the big piles of garbage bags that Afroz and his volunteers had filled with trash. Slowly, that immense trash pile began to reduce, revealing the sand and rocks underneath.

Afroz celebrated 100 weeks of cleaning, and the country cheered him on. But then there was a snag. The municipality trucks stopped collecting the heaps of filled bags. Frustrated, Afroz said he was going to stop cleaning the beach if the municipality wouldn't help. There was such outrage at the thought of him stopping such a noble task that the authorities stepped in and promised that the trucks would continue to come, as long as the work was ongoing.

So, Afroz agreed to carry on, and after three years, or 160 weeks, the beach was finally clean.

In March 2018, turtles came back to the beach for the first time in twenty years to lay their eggs.

Afroz was so proud of completing this mammoth task with such excellent results, that he is now working on cleaning up the longest river in Mumbai, the Mithi.

The Greta Effect:
Climate Change Warrior
A Growth Mindset Case Study

- - - - - - - - - - - - - - - - - - - -

Almost everyone in the world knows Greta Thunberg. Before she was sixteen, she inspired children all over the world to hold climate change protests to make their governments pay attention. But did you know that at first, no one listened to her?

Greta was always interested in climate change, and worried about adults not doing anything to fix the problem. She wrote an essay (which won a competition) about feeling unsafe because of climate change. She tried to raise interest about climate change, but no one really did anything. So, she did it herself. She would sit outside the Swedish parliament with a sign that said: "School strike for Climate Change" all by herself — every school day for three whole weeks.

At first, she must have felt very small and all alone. But the newspapers discovered her, and she became quite famous. But even while people were talking about her, and beginning to talk about climate change, there were even more people who tried to ignore what she was saying. They claimed that her parents were making her do it. They said that her autism meant she didn't really understand how the world worked.

They said she was just a little girl. And they said that she should be in school learning, and not bothering the adults!
But Greta stayed calm and focused on her message.
She talked to the United Nations, she talked to the US government, and she went on television shows all over the world, making the point that climate change was here, it was real, and that something needed to be done about it.

And finally, people started to listen.

And that is a very good example of a Growth Mindset. Greta wanted to make a change, she thought about how to do it, and got some ideas. She tried out the ideas, and it was hard at first, but she stuck to it. And finally, she succeeded in getting her message out all over the world.

And while climate change is still a problem, governments are now working on finding solutions for some of the causes of climate change.

Growth Mindset
YOU!

- - - - - - - - - - - - - - - - -

Think about the two case studies.
Did you notice that both people felt inspired to do the thing that
made them a superhero in their own way?
And that each of them had to overcome problems in order to be
taken seriously?

Think back to your dream. Do you know how to achieve it? What
challenges might you face?

	Afroz Shah	Greta Thunberg	Now its your turn!
What they should have done	Practiced law, enjoyed his beachside flat	Stayed in school, was quiet	
What they did	Cleaned up the beach for a very long time	Campaigned to raise awareness of the climate emergency	
What made them a superhero?	A desire to improve the beach, love of nature and beautiful things	Understanding that no one was really trying to fix things, a desire to enforce clean-up processes	
What could/did they do next?	Began to clean up a long (and very dirty) river	Did very well in her school exams, traveled all over the world, continued to raise awareness, and is looking into improving farming practices	
Their Growth Mindset skills	Determination, compassion, love of nature	Determination, good sense of humor, drive to succeed	

Did you notice how both people in the case studies were determined to succeed in their mission?

Another excellent example of such determination is the Olympic sprinter, Morolake Akinosun.

In 2011, she tweeted that:

Morolake Akinsun
@Morolake Akinsun

In 2016, I will be 22, graduated from a school I have not chosen yet, and going to the Olympics.

March 2011

In 2016, she tweeted:

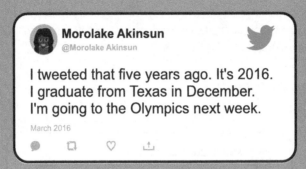

Morolake Akinsun
@Morolake Akinsun

I tweeted that five years ago. It's 2016.
I graduate from Texas in December.
I'm going to the Olympics next week.

March 2016

Colour the picture below of Morolake Akinsun winning her race.

Reading these two messages, one after the other like this, makes it seem as though she is very lucky. But in fact, what is not made clear in those messages is what she was doing before the first message and in between the two of them. She was working very hard, both at her sprinting and at her schoolwork. She had a dream, and she was determined to make that dream come true.

Think SMART for a Growth Mindset

Remember the exercise on page 75 when you wrote down your dream and goals and how to achieve them? It's time to update them.

Now is the time to be specific by completing the activity below. You can use your vision board to help you.

It's your turn to think SMART!

My Goal: _____

What steps do i need to take to achieve this goal:

1 _____
2 _____
3 _____

Why do I want to accomplish this goal?
_____
_____
_____

How long will it take me to reach this goal?
_____
_____

What help do I need? Who can help me achieve this goal?
_____
_____
_____

Think SMART

- - - - - - - - - - - - - - - - - - -

Thinking SMART is something that everyone can use every time they
want to achieve something. It is a way of working out what you need
to do, and how to achieve your goal, or set a series of milestones
towards that goal. For example, if you want to be a doctor, you will
need very good school marks, and will need to meet certain criteria
to get into medical school.

You will need to be good with blood and yucky stuff. You will need to take four years of college classes, four years of medical school, then another three to seven years in a residency program (when you work as a doctor in your chosen specialization) before you are a fully qualified doctor.

Thinking SMART will help you realize that becoming a doctor will take at least ten years or so, which gives you a potential timeline to achieve your goal.

Let's look at it in more detail:
SMART:

SPECIFIC: Be precise in your dream. "I want to be a doctor, specializing in childhood medicine" not "I want to heal people." "I want to be in the 20__ Olympics for long-distance freestyle swimming," not "I want an Olympic medal."

MEASURABLE: If your dream is to be famous, for example, you must decide if you want to be well-known in your hometown, your state, the country, or in the whole world.

state

country

hometown

whole world

ACHIEVABLE: Being famous in your hometown is much easier than being famous throughout the whole world. If your dream is to win your hometowns' annual marathon, for example, you are unlikely to gain worldwide fame for that (going viral on social media notwithstanding! But that is usually because something unusual happens, apart from just winning the race!).

REALISTIC: If you want to be a renowned artist, hoping to have your picture hung in the finest art galleries in the world, but you are not very artistic to start with, then this may seem unrealistic. But you can keep working on your art, looking at what other artists are producing, and improving your own skills — and one day, who knows?

TIMEBOUND: Most dreams come with an expiration date, but not all of them.

Some of those that do include doing sports at the highest levels: if you have not achieved your goals by the time you are forty, for example, you are unlikely to be chosen for your local team. This means you will have to adjust your goals: a smaller league, a "veterans" group (designed for older people, not former soldiers!), or changing your dream from performing to coaching.

Other dreams are not timebound at all: eighty-year-old grandmothers have gone back to school for their undergraduate degrees, writers can be any age at all, and even actors can be pensioners — some of the roles for grouchy grandpas or lovely grandmas can be great fun. Whether your dream is timebound or not, do try to work out a completion timetable: we humans like to have a schedule to follow, even if it is one that we have made up ourselves!

Resilience:
Bouncing Back

Sometimes, no matter how determined we are, things can go wrong.

Physical things that go wrong can include an athlete getting hurt before a big race or match.

Emotional things that go wrong can include getting bad news that distracts the hero from their purpose.

Mental things that go wrong can include getting very tired, suffering from anxiety, or having panic attacks.

Physical

Emotional

Mental

For example:

• When Afroz realized the trash bags weren't being collected, he became angry and threatened to stop doing his clean-up work.
• When people told Greta that she should be in school, that she didn't understand enough about the world, or made fun of her (or, worse, pitied her!) for having autism, she didn't whine or throw a tantrum.

INSTEAD:
• Afroz continued his good work when public opinion was so much in his favor.
• And Greta dealt with the "haters" with such calmness and a good sense of humor that even more people began to support her.

But both of them had moments when it just seemed too hard to keep going.

Every superhero has an "I can't": a supervillain who is out to make them fail.
Moments when you feel like you cannot go on, are when your secret superhero's nemesis is trying to take control.

This is when you can use meditation, empathy, and other skills you have learned in this book to regain your calm and refocus.

The good news is that there are many ways to cope with your secret villain, just as there are many ways to make your secret superhero bigger and stronger.

Let us take a look at some more ways to cope, along with a brand-new Storytime!

"Storytime: Compassion, Kindness And Self-Acceptance"

"I'm going to be a successful businesswoman one day!" said Joanne to her mom.

"That's nice, love," replied her mom, bustling around the kitchen.

"You? Don't make me laugh."

Oh no! It was Peter, Joanne's older brother. He was mean. Sometimes he could be nice, but most of the time he laughed at Joanne. He would tease her too, hiding her books and toys up high, where she couldn't reach them.

If Joanne had known that Peter was at home, she wouldn't have said anything about her dream.

"Don't be mean, Peter," warned Mom, taking a steaming hot lasagna out of the oven.

"Why? She's not going to be a businesswoman, she's just a squirt." Peter was grinning at Joanne.

She glared at him. "I am too. I'm not going to be small forever, you know!"

"You're never going to get as big as me, are you?"

"I might!"

"Nah, you won't. Will she, Mom?"

"Peter, you can be so mean to Joanne sometimes, you know that?"
Then Mom turned to Joanne: "Boys do tend to be taller than girls
when they're adults, and I'm only short myself. You probably won't
be as big as Peter, I'm sorry."

Joanne fought back tears. She was sick of being small!

But then she had an idea!
"Well, I might not be big, but I'm already cleverer than you!" she
said to her brother. "You've never even read a book in your life!"
Mom said, "Joanne! Don't be mean to your brother!"
Peter was so surprised that he just sat there, staring at Joanne, who
stuck her tongue out at him when Mom turned away for a moment.

Joanne glared at her brother and was very surprised to see that he looked... sad. She felt bad, as though she had done something naughty. Mom turned around, holding the garlic bread, and looked from Peter to Joanne.

"What's going on?" she asked, looking worried.

"Nothing..." said Peter quickly.

Just then, Dad got home, and they all sat at the dinner table and ate their meal.

Mom and Dad chatted about their workdays, neither of them seeming to notice that Peter was being very quiet — which was unlike him! Joanne watched her brother as she ate. Later, Mom and Dad told them to work together to clear the table. Joanne stood up and began to carry the plates to the kitchen, scraping the scraps into the garbage disposal before stacking them into the dishwasher.

To her surprise, Peter brought the rest of the plates and joined her. He usually waited until Mom and Dad were watching TV, then went upstairs, leaving her to do the dishes by herself.

"So," he said, "What's your business idea?"

Joanne was suspicious. "Why? So you can tease me about it?"

Peter blushed. "No... I'm interested." He paused for a moment and then added, "You were right."

"I don't read much. I don't like it, it's hard. The words kind of... wiggle on the page. Doesn't that happen to you?"

Joanne glanced at him. He was very red, and although he was trying to keep his voice casual, she could tell he really wanted to hear her answer. She turned away to put the last dish in the machine, and said, "No, the words are fine."

Now it was her turn to hesitate. "Peter?"

"Mmm?"

"Have you ever been tested for dyslexia?"

"What's that? No, I don't think so. Why?"

"My friend has it. She struggled with reading too, and they said she has it. It's a learning difficulty."

"Are you saying I'm dumb?" Peter tried to sound angry, but he couldn't quite pull it off.

"No, of course not. My friend's not dumb! She's brilliant at math, she can add up in her head better than the teacher, and she remembers everything she's told, and she can sing really well —"

"Okay, okay!" Peter was laughing and seemed very relieved. "I'm good at math too! Do you think I might have this... dys... what was it?"

"Dyslexia. You might," said Joanne. "Have you always struggled with reading?"

"Yeah…" Peter shrugged. "I just couldn't get it. Weird, though, when teacher read out to us, I was fine. I could understand the story and answer the questions. But when I couldn't do the same with my reading book, she got mad at me. So… I pretended I didn't care."
"Why didn't you ask for help?"

Peter blushed again. "I thought everyone hated reading, really. That they were just pretending and that they'd… I dunno, cheated somehow to get the answers."
Joanne turned to look at her brother, her face full of sympathy. "That must've sucked."

Peter had that same look as before, sad, and thoughtful. "It… it wasn't fun. That's why I always pick on you. If Mom's shouting at me for picking on you, she's not shouting at me for not doing my homework." He gave her a shamefaced grin.

"That's terrible! Peter, you must tell Mom! And your teachers. There are programs and assistance for people with dyslexia —"
"No!" said Peter. "I'm not going to tell anyone. I don't want to be teased."
Joanne gave Peter a look.
"And don't give me that 'Mom' look either. I can't tell them, not after all this time. They'll wonder why I never said anything."

"They probably will wonder, Peter. I'm wondering myself! But they'll help you, they really will."

"I'm not telling them!" Peter turned and stormed out of the kitchen. Joanne looked after him thoughtfully. He said he wasn't telling them, but there was something he hadn't said...

Joanne went into the living room, her heart beating hard. "Mom, Dad," she said. "Can I speak to you for a moment?"

Mom paused the movie they were watching. "What is it?" she asked. "Is it your brother bullying you again?" She began to get up. "I'll ground him —"

"No, Mom," said Joanne quickly. "It is about Peter, but he's not bullying me. I know why he does bully me though. That's what I want to talk to you about."

Mom and Dad leaned forward, and Joanne told them about what Peter had said in the kitchen. As she spoke, Joanne heard Peter's door open upstairs. He didn't come down, though, and she imagined him standing by his door, listening hard. As she had suspected: he hadn't told her not to tell their parents, because he had hoped that she would explain it all to Mom and Dad. Relieved, she carried on, finishing with, "and I think he has dyslexia, like my friend at school."

There was a small silence when she finished speaking, except for a creak from an upstairs floorboard.

"Oh, my goodness…" said Mom, and Joanne saw there were tears in her eyes.

"I scolded him about his grades," said Dad, his normally cheery face solemn and dismayed.

Joanne tried to reassure them. "He was trying to hide it from you. It's not your fault."

Mom waved a hand. "But we should have realized something was going on."

The next morning, when Mom took them to school, she parked the car and got out with them.

"What's happening?" asked Peter.

Mom patted his arm. "Son, why didn't you tell us you were struggling with reading?"

Peter blushed and shook his head. "What are you going to do?" he asked.

"Speak to your teacher," said Mom. "We should have realized you were struggling, but your teacher also should have picked up that there was a problem!"

"Oh…" said Peter, but he seemed hopeful. Joanne smiled as she ran off to her class.

The next few weeks were very busy. Mom and Peter spent hours together, reading through books. Peter was given books printed on different colored paper, he was given special sunglasses to wear when reading, and he was praised and encouraged every time he made progress.

Joanne would sit with him sometimes, reading her own book, and seeing his clenched hands, sweating face, and straining eyes as he wrestled to make sense of the words that were so easy for Joanne.

She learned how to help him, giving him time to sound out the letters, and she applauded him when he mastered a new word. With the help of his teachers, parents, sister, and the dyslexia specialist at school, he was soon making good progress. One day he closed his book with a relieved sigh and turned to Joanne.

"I'll may never be a great reader," he said. "But my therapist told me something that made me feel much more confident."
"What's that?" asked Joanne.

"Dyslexia is caused by having a brain that works differently from the way other brains do. That's why I'm really good at some things, but not so great with reading. I'm not dumb, I'm unique and have many other strengths!

"I knew that!" said Joanne, hugging his arm. "I probably won't be able to go to college, though," he said sadly. Joanne looked at him. "Firstly, yes, you will!

They have dyslexia help at colleges, too, you know. Plus, there are plenty of apps and dictation devices you can use that write for you by using your voice. There are plenty of courses for jobs that don't need a lot of reading. Besides, I thought you wanted to be a mechanic?"

"How do you know that?" Peter was surprised.

Joanne shrugged. "I heard you talking to your friend the other day. Being a mechanic is a cool job, you'd be amazing at it, and it pays well. You don't need to go to college if you don't want to."
"Tell that to Mom and Dad..." said Peter glumly.

"No," said Joanne calmly. "you tell them. They'll understand, I'm sure they will. Besides, Mom never went to college."
"How do you know that?" Peter was astonished: he had always thought both his parents went to college!

"Her dad wouldn't let her. He said it was for boys only. But times have changed, so I'll go to college, and you don't have to, how's that?"

Peter laughed. "Sounds good to me. Thanks for being such a cool little sister."

"You're very welcome," said Joanne, demurely. "You can do the dishes tonight, to make up for all the times you made me do them alone!"

"Deal!" Peter grinned.

Mindfulness, kindness and compassion

Sometimes people who are smaller than others can feel as though they are not as important as those big, tall people. If you are on the short side, just remember, you didn't do anything to deserve being small, just as tall people didn't do anything special or clever to get those longer legs! What is important is the kind of person you are. Being mean might feel satisfying for a moment, but upsetting people is hardly ever much fun, no matter how much they seem to deserve it!

If you are being bullied or feel that you are being bullied (they are not always the same thing, but both instances are upsetting), there are some ways to cope.

Bullying is when people hurt you physically or emotionally, calling you names, hitting you, taking, breaking, or hiding your belongings, or teasing you.

Feeling as though you are being bullied can happen when people do things like:

- Ask you intrusive questions
- Sit too close to you
- Follow you around

If you are not sure how to stand up for yourself, this sort of behavior can feel a lot like bullying, but the person concerned might not realize that it is upsetting. They might want to be friends with you, and so they ask questions. They might come from a different culture, where people tend to sit closer than other cultures feel is polite or necessary.

They might be new to the school and not sure of where to go, so they have decided following you is the safe thing for them to do.

If it is this sort of annoyance, usually explaining that you feel uncomfortable and asking them politely not to ask questions like that, sit a little further away, or bring their own book to read, will be enough for them to stop. If they are worried about getting lost, perhaps put up with it for a little while, just until they know their way around! Knowing the reason they are following you will usually put your mind at ease!

Standing up for yourself in this way is called "setting boundries" Boundries are very healthy to have. It's like having a line that people know they cant cross and that you don't let people cross either. Boundries can help keep you feeling safe, so always voice them when you are feeling like they are being crossed.

Now onto the serious bullying. Bullies are people who have let their inside villain beat their secret superhero. They like to make people feel bad, and they laugh when they see people cry because of things they've done. Very often, bullies have reasons for being a bully, sometimes very sad ones, sometimes rather silly ones. But sometimes, they don't realize that they are being horrible — they think they are "playing" or "teasing", or that it is "just a joke".

These reasons do not make it right, and you do not have to let it continue.

Act brave. Set a boundary, and ignore the bully. Firmly and clearly tell the bully to stop, then walk away. Doing this is called setting your boundary. Practice ways to ignore the hurtful remarks, like acting uninterested. By ignoring the bully, you're showing that you don't care. Eventually, the bully will probably get bored with trying to bother you.

Tell an adult. Teachers, principals, and parents can all help stop bullying.

Talk about it. Talk to someone you trust, such as a guidance counselor, teacher, sibling, or friend. They may offer some helpful suggestions. Even if they can't fix the situation, it may help you feel a little less alone.

It can be tempting to "get even" with the bully, but try not to do this. If you hurt them, you will be the one in the wrong — plus, it really doesn't feel good to cause pain in others! Humiliating them will only make them hate you and is very unlikely to stop their bullying ways — it can even make them worse.

Make sure your secret superhero keeps you doing the right thing all the time.

Mindfulness: Being fully Present

Being mindful doesn't mean being perfect. No one is perfect, no one at all! Once you accept that fact, you will find that everything becomes a little easier. So many people try to pretend that everything is perfect, and that can be very tiring:

- Pretending to know everything.
- Pretending to have things they do not have or cannot afford.
- Pretending to be someone that they are not.

Adults are not perfect either - a big part of being a grown-up is learning to accept yourself and the situation just as it is and make the most of every day by living in the moment.

Everyone has lazy days when they don't want to do anything, even if they have quite a lot to do. And everyone has bad days when everything is annoying, and their mood is low.

And that is okay. There are ways to cope with these grouchy days. So here are some tips on how to improve your mood and accept yourself, flaws and all!

- Do something fun – draw a picture, write a letter to your friend, or build a tower out of blocks. This can take your mind off whatever makes you grumpy, and you will soon cheer up by doing something you enjoy.

- Remind yourself that there are more than eight billion people on Earth, and every single one has made a mistake, felt silly or small, or embarrassed themselves in some way: it is normal to have grumpy moments!

- Be as kind to yourself as you would be to a stranger. You wouldn't shout at them for accidents or not scoring well when they've tried hard – so don't do it to yourself either!

- Do some exercise. Our bodies are designed to work in harmony: body, mind, and soul. So, if your emotions are sad, sometimes exercising your body can help. Your brain produces hormones when you exercise that are referred to as 'feel-good' hormones because they make you feel happy. Or happier, at least!

Self Compassion

- -

Do you spend ages looking at social media or magazines, wondering how the models came to be so pretty and slim and elegant? Do you watch sports games or athletics and wish you were like those muscular people, so confident in their own skills? Do you sometimes feel like you don't really fit into your class, your school, your peer group? Stop!

The more you think about things that you might be doing wrong, the more things you will find to be upset about. And this is not because there are hundreds of flaws to be found, it is because you are telling your brain to find something wrong, so it is coming up with all sorts of silly things!

Really, no one cares if your nose is a bit big — you'll grow into it. No one minds if you are slow at answering the math problem for the teacher — most of them are just glad it's not them! And if you find that everyone really is much better than you are at things, there might be a learning difficulty that is holding you back.

Don't be scared to ask for help — it's not your fault and the sooner you ask help, the sooner you will learn new ways and skills to support yourself and succeed.

Diva Time!

Everyone has grumpy days sometimes, and if they only happen once in a while, you can give in to them. Spend a few hours sulking in your room; go and read a book in the park, ignoring everyone; or even have a good cry (yes, even if you are a boy!)

But the problem with bad moods is that they can become a habit. If you are upset because you have had a setback — a fight with a friend, your grades weren't as good as you had hoped, you didn't make it into the school play — allow yourself a set time for being a 'diva'. Say, "I've failed my test, I'm really mad because I studied very hard, and I'm going to sulk about it for twelve hours." And then set a timer for those twelve hours.

During that time, you can moan about the test, complain that the teacher wasn't fair, and sulk because your hard work wasn't good enough this time. But when the twelve hours are up and 'diva time' is over, the test is forgotten! Stop talking about it, tell yourself to work even harder next time, and come up with a plan to ace the next test.

By allowing yourself 'diva time', you are acknowledging that you were upset, you are giving yourself time to grieve for that missed target — but, by setting a time limit for it, you are not allowing yourself to wallow in it for too long.

Spending too long looking back at one failed test will disrupt your learning — that's why it is a strictly limited period of time.

Move On
Don't dwell on mistakes you have made, or tests you've failed. Be your own best friend. If you are not sure of how hard to be on yourself, pretend to be your own secret superhero. When you make a mistake, it can be tempting to beat yourself up, call yourself names, be mean, or let yourself think that you will never make it.

But imagine that your superhero has come to you, upset because they have made that same mistake. Would you scold them? Would you call them names? Would you be mean to them? Would you tell them to give up on their dreams? Of course not!

So why would you treat yourself worse than your secret superhero? You would give them a hug, let them pour out their distress, and you would comfort them, telling them they've got this, they'll get it next time, and that it's no big deal really.

Tell yourself the same things, and you'll soon feel better — and your secret superhero will be stronger and better than ever! And you will be able to move on from that setback.

Creativity for Growth

Living mindfully is not all about just being good and not having fun. Living mindfully includes enjoying as much of life as you can, and that means making time for things that make you happy.
It doesn't matter if you are good at everything or not. Try new things if they look interesting to you. Learning new things keeps your brain active and can stave off boredom and glum feelings.

It doesn't have to be a big thing: learn how to say "thank you" in Chinese one day, learn how to sew on a button the next. Learning a bunch of little things will help to boost your self-confidence — and might encourage you to learn big things, like how to speak Chinese, or sew a whole outfit!

Draw a picture every day for a month and see how good you have gotten by the end — or just draw because you like it. Or buy yourself a coloring book. Coloring books are not just for little kids — many adults love them too!

Date: ___ / ___ / ___

Today I feel:

 Sad Angry Sick Meh

 Okay All Right  Pretty Good Good Awesome!

Because:

_____

_____

Three GOOD things that happened today!

1 _____ 2 _____ 3 _____

Today: I am GRATEFUL for:

_____

_____

Tomorrow: I am LOOKING FORWARD to:

_____

_____

Reflecting on your journal

A good tip for those grumpy days we mentioned earlier is to use your journaling pages to record things that happened in your day. At the end of every day, write down at least one and up to five good things that happened that day. It could be something like: "Snuggled with Mom after dinner," or "We went to see a movie: it was great!" Make sure you do it every day, and then when you are having a grumpy day, flip back the pages and read through those good memories. They will make you smile, and your secret superhero becomes even stronger when you are happy, and he or she will chase away the grumps in no time!

Make a List!

Lists are your friend when you are trying to achieve your dream. As well as writing down your dreams and how you will achieve them, you can make lists of:

• Your support network - make a list of all the people that are there to support you or that you can go to when you hit an obstacle. Having this list handy when you do hit a bump in the road will remind you that you are not alone and that there are people you can go to for help.

• How to ground yourself when you are anxious: take deep, slow breaths, and count five things you can see, four things you can hear, three things you can touch, two things you can smell, and one thing you can taste. By the time you get to the last one, you should be calmer.

• Write down things that have gone wrong (after Diva Time) and then tear them up! They are gone!

Congratulations!

Finally, draw a picture of yourself once again. Draw yourself as your secret superhero! Don't forget your supersuit! And also draw all the villains that you have defeated: worry, lack of confidence, doubt. You are a wonderful superhero! Now turn to that very first picture of yourself and see how much you have changed as you have worked your way through this journal.

Well done!
you have filled in your first journal!

TODAY IS: _____

Draw your day in this box.

write a little about your day. Try to include three **GOOD** thing

_____

_____

_____

_____

TODAY'S DATE: _____ / _____ / _____

One great thing happened today! It was _____
_____
_____
_____

TODAY I FELT:

TODAY:

- ( ) I was CURIOUS
- ( ) I SOLVED a problem
- ( ) I WORKED on something difficult
- ( ) I ASKED for help
- ( ) I SLEPT well
- ( ) _____

What's Next??

Get featured on our Instagram page by sending or tagging us in your photos of yourself and your journal!

Now it's time to get more journaling pages!

You can ask a parent or adult to log onto our website where you will be able to purchase more downloadable journaling pages to print at home.

Alternatively, it's time to order a new Daily Journal. Link can also be found on the website.

🌐 www.mymindfulco.com   📷 mymindfulco

DEDICATION

This journal is dedicated to all my boys. Thank you for being my guides and biggest teachers.

I love you.

From Mom

Made in the USA
Coppell, TX
01 December 2023

25108027R00098